MW01244107

Day Hiking Trails of

Gooseberry Falls State Park

By Rob Bignell

Atiswinic Press · Ojai, Calif.

DAY HIKING TRAILS OF GOOSEBERRY FALLS STATE PARK

A GUIDEBOOK IN THE
HITTIN' THE TRAIL: MINNESOTA SERIES

Copyright Rob Bignell, 2016

Atiswinic Press
Ojai, Calif. 93023
inventingreality.4t.com/writingaffirmations.html

ISBN 978-0-9961625-3-1

Cover photo of Upper Falls in autumn
Back cover photo by Bryan Bignell

Manufactured in the United States of America
First printing May 2016

For Kieran

Contents

Introduction

I magine a place where five waterfalls spill over billion-year-old rock, all within a mile of one another, where both incredible vistas of the world's largest freshwater lake and paths past an array of sweet-scented wildflowers await, where you can traipse through historic handcrafted stone buildings or alongside a creek meandering about an evergreen forest. The place is real: It's called Gooseberry Falls State Park, which many consider the crown jewel of Minnesota's multitude of natural gems.

Located along the North Shore about 30 miles northeast of Duluth, Gooseberry Falls is an outdoor recreational paradise. Minnesota's second most visited state park, it's popular among hikers, campers and nature lovers of all stripes. With about 630,000 annual visitors, more people visit Gooseberry Falls than half of all national parks.

Geology

Gooseberry Falls' great scenery would not exist but not for 1.1-billion-year-old lava flows that formed when North America began to separate into two, forming what today is called the Mid-Continent Rift. The rift extends all across the Great Lakes to as far south as Kansas.

In Minnesota, those volcanic flows along Lake Superior are known as the North Shore Volcanic Group. With lava flows occurring over millions of years, they can run up to 30,000 feet in the region. Locally, the basalt rocks that create the park's waterfalls are referred to as the Gooseberry Lavas.

Fast forward to 10,000 A.D. After eons of being buried by sediment, the great glaciers of the last ice age scraped off most of the terrain, leaving only the basalt and a thin layer of till over it. Cold Lake Superior is merely what remains of a melted glacier in a low spot of the Precambrian-era rift, and the rivers along the North Shore are carving through the remaining till and sediment until reaching the underlying basalt.

Geography

Three general landscapes dominate the picturesque park.

The first is the shoreline with Lake Superior that largely runs south of Minn. Hwy. 61. Outcroppings of the ancient 1.1-billion-year-old basalt are common just above the waterline. The **Picnic Flow Trail** is an excellent route to explore the park's shoreline.

The second zone are the highlands rising sharply above the shore, mainly north of Hwy. 61. A variety of trees grow along the hills as the elevation changes, resulting in a range of micro ecosystems. The **Superior Hiking Trail** heads into and atop those highlands in the park.

A third zone is the Gooseberry River itself, which forms a gorge cutting through the hills and then flows in a shallow cut through the shoreline area. Rather than replicate the surrounding hills or shoreline, the river with its five waterfalls creates its own unique environment for plants. Two good trails to discover all the river has to offer is the **Gooseberry River Trail** and the **River View Trail**, the latter of which heads to the park's iconic waterfalls.

History

Most people visit the state park for its fantastic set of waterfalls. But a number of trails also explore the area's fascinating history.

Native Americans, including the Cree, Dakotah and Ojibwe, have long resided in what is now the state park. The river naturally attracted a variety of game and offered a good spot to fish.

French explorers Médard Chouart des Groseilliers (The anglization of his name, "Mr. Gooseberry," appears in English texts of the time.) and Pierre-Esprit Radisson were the first Europeans to pass the area in the mid 1600s. They claimed the region for France, which lost it to the British in 1763. The burgeoning United States won the territory in 1783.

More than another century would pass, though, before American settlers and pioneers began to harness the North Shore's great resources. Most notably for what is now Gooseberry Falls State Park, in 1900 the Nestor Logging Co. set up its headquarters at the mouth of the Gooseberry River and built a railroad – the Nestor Grade – to remove the vast white pine forest stretching across the Arrowhead. Most of the logs were rafted over Lake Superior to sawmills in Wisconsin and Michigan. By the 1920s, though, the white pine forests were gone. Signs of that logging era can be found on the **River View Trail**.

Despite the then barren landscape, North Shore residents hoped tourism would make up for the collapsed logging industry. Their efforts paid off, and by 1933 the state voted to preserve the area that makes up the state park. The Civilian Conservation Corps built roads, trails, a campground, a picnic area, and a visitor center; the structures are notable for their use of red, blue, brown and black basalt in the construction. In 1937, the state park was established. Many of the beautiful, handcrafted stone buildings erected by the

CCC can be seen on the **CCC Buildings Trail**.

The park was named for the river, but the origin of the waterway's name remains somewhat unclear. Some say the riverway was named for des Groseilliers while others believe it's a translation of the Ojibwe word Shab-on-im-i-kan-i-sibi, the gooseberry plant that grows along the riverbanks. Those berry bushes can be seen on the **Gooseberry River Trail**.

Today, the park stands at 1,682 acres in size. In addition to the waterfalls, Lake Superior scenery, and CCC buildings, the Joseph N. Alexander Visitor Center, erected in 1996, also is a draw; among its most popular interpretive displays is that of the Dire Wolf, a freakishly large stuffed male wolf that died in the area during 1991.

When to Visit

The best months to day hike Gooseberry Falls State Park and nearby trails are mid-May through September. Depending on the year, April and October also can be pleasant.

During spring, waterfalls run at their highest levels, the bird migration is in full swing, and bugs are nil. Trails can be muddy, though, as snow typically melts between April and early May.

Unlike the rest of Minnesota, summers at Gooseberry Falls usually are not hot, as cool breezes off Lake Superior keep heat and most insects at bay. Rain, however, can occur during the afternoon even when the morning is sunny, so always check the weather forecast before heading out.

For many hikers, autumn marks the best time to hit a Gooseberry Falls trail. By mid-August, summer's bugs are gone, trails mostly are dry, and throughout September maples and aspen light the wilderness with color. A sweatshirt often is needed during the day, though, and nights can be chilly.

Mid-October through March usually is too cold and wet for day hiking. Once snow falls, trails typically are used for cross-country skiing, snowmobiling or snowshoeing.

If camping, be sure to reserve sites several months out, as Gooseberry State Park is very popular.

How to Get There

Several major highways offer access to Gooseberry Falls. All converge in Duluth, and from there, it's roughly 25 miles north via Minn. Hwy. 61 to Two Harbors and then another 13 miles north to the state park.

From the Minneapolis-St. Paul area, take Interstate 35 to Duluth. Where I-35 ends, the road becomes Hwy. 61. If in northern Minnesota, take either U.S. Hwy. 2 or U.S. Hwy 53 to Duluth.

If in northern or eastern Wisconsin, U.S. Hwys. 45 and 51 as well as Wis. Hwy. 13 all lead to Hwy. 2, which leads west to Duluth. From western Wisconsin, U.S. Hwy. 63 as well as Wis. Hwy. 35 both head north to Hwy. 2. Hwy. 53 runs from Interstate 94 at Eau Claire into Duluth; it's the only combination of four-lane highways connecting most of Wisconsin to the North Shore.

Maps

To properly prepare for any hike, you should examine maps before hitting the trail and bring them with you (see the Special Section for more). No guidebook can reproduce a map as well as the satellite pictures or topographical maps that you can find online for free. To that end, the companion website to this book offers (*hikeswithtykes.com/headintothe cabin_trailmaps.html*) a variety of printable maps for each listed trail.

Gooseberry Falls State Park

Gooseberry Falls State Park largely can be divided into three distinct areas. The most popular section of the park is south of the Gooseberry River, where trails leading to the waterfalls, the visitor center, and the campground are located. Less visited is the section north of the river and east of Minn. Hwy. 61, which has only two walking paths but great views of Lake Superior and historic structures. Visitors can find solitude in the section west of Hwy. 61, in which a number of trails heads into the highlands overlooking Lake Superior.

River View Trail

Three waterfalls and an agate beach await day hikers on the park's River View Trail.

The route, as described here, runs about 1.8 miles total through the heart of what many consider to be among the most beautiful parks on the North Shore, if not all of Minnesota.

Upon entering the state park, leave your vehicle in the first lot. Take the connector trail northeast to a walkway, on which you'll go left/north.

A mixed evergreen, aspen, birch forest covers the park. As hiking, don't be surprised to find enormous stumps – they're the remains of white pines that once covered the North Shore until logged off in the 1890s.

Upper, Middle, Lower Falls

At the next junction, go right/northeast. When the path splits, continue right. This leads to Gooseberry River and the Lower Falls.

A 30-foot drop, Lower Falls is the last of the waterfalls before the river flows into Lake Superior. The Gooseberry rushes over volcanic rock formed 1.1 billion years ago when lava flows covered this part of the earth; today, they are the black rock visible at each of the falls. When glaciers retreated about 10,000 years ago at the end of the last ice age, erosion exposed the hardened volcanic bedrock, creating the waterfalls.

The view of Lower Falls technically places you on the River View Trail. Walk left/northwest; within a few feet, you'll come to Middle Falls, another 30-foot drop.

Continue northeast under the highway bridge, staying on the trail that hugs the shoreline. You'll quickly arrive at Upper Falls, the third 30-foot drop on the river.

Common loons and ravens often can be spotted circling the pools beneath the falls while herring gulls nest in colonies along the lakeshore. Each spring and fall, migratory birds using the North Shore flyway arrive here in great numbers.

Backtrack to the highway, this time crossing the river via the catwalk under the bridge to the other side. Continue heading southeast, again passing Middle Falls. This side of the Gooseberry affords a better view of Lower Falls.

Agate Beach

At the next junction, continue straight, crossing the footbridge onto an island in the river's middle. Stay on the trail hugging the island's shoreline then cross the next bridge to the river's south shore.

Go left/southeast, following the trail along the river to its mouth with Lake Superior. You'll soon reach Agate Beach, where you can hunt for agates on the rocky shoreline and explore tide pools in which tadpoles often can be found.

Sometimes various species of Lake Superior salmon can be spotted in the river. Black bears, gray wolves, and whitetail deer also call the park home.

Follow the river upstream. About a half-mile from beach, take the connecting trail left/southeast and at the next trail junction go right/southwest for the parking lots.

Picnic Flow Trail

Day hikers can walk an expansive cliff of billion-year-old lava rock overlooking Lake Superior via the Picnic Flow Trail.

The 3-mile round-trip heads to an impressive part of the state park that most visitors miss. The Picnic Flow is worth the hike, however. It'll give you the feeling of being on the moon – or if a good wind is blowing off the lake, of being on newly formed volcanic rock in Hawaii.

Use the same parking lot as for the River Trail near the visitor's center. Leave from the lot's northeast corner, heading into a birch and spruce woods where the trail veers south, quickly crossing Camp Road near the camp registration pullout.

Once on the road's other side, continue south into a grassy area of asters, buttercups, daisies, hawkweed and Metensia. The varied colors of these wildflowers – white, yellow, orange and blue – can make for a nice show amid the green grass.

At the grassy area's south end, take the paved Gitchi-Gami State Trail right/east through the woods and to a parking lot for the Bird Ridge Group site where campers unload their vehicles. A path leads from the lot's southeast side to just north of where Pebble Creek flows into Lake Superior. Go right/southeast at the trail intersection.

In about 400 feet, the path opens onto the Picnic Lava Flow. About 1.1 billion years ago, red hot lava spread across this area in smooth and ropy swaths called a Pahoehoe flow. Such flows are common in Hawaii today. Follow this ancient basalt northeast along the lakeshore; sometimes the trail winds into the woods, especially at small bays.

Looking down at your feet, keep an eye out for amygdules, which usually are banded blues and creams and reddish-whites. These round rocks were weathered out of the basalt and can be up to a quarter in size. The white crystals in the rock are feldspar that can be up to 2 inches wide. Remember to look up, though – a steep cliff overlooks Lake Superior to the east.

Water puddles here may look like tidal pools that are common on Pacific Northwest coasts, but they're not formed the same way. Instead, splash water gets trapped here during storms and remains until evaporating.

Despite a moon-like barrenness, the Picnic Lava Flow is home to plants including harebells and cinquefoil.

Once the lava flow ends, the trail heads through a grassy area and grove of mountain ash. It then comes to Agate Beach II, where orange lichen covers the bedrock. Tansies, wild roses and raspberry bushes also flourish here.

Take the stairs to the rock picnic shelter. On the shelter's right is a sea stack in the making. Common in the Pacific Northwest, wave action creates sea stacks by separating chunks of rock from the mainland.

The overlook with the picnic shelter sits amid red pine. It offers a good view of the lake with its waves striking black basalt. When windy, the waves turn a frothy white.

A spit to the shelter's north comes and goes seasonally as the lake's breaking waves carry sand and pebbles beyond the bar while the Gooseberry River's currents bring their own sediment downstream. The two mix, forming the bar in summer through autumn with the river's heavier flow in spring washing it away.

After taking in the sights from the shelter, turn back here and retrace your steps to the parking lot.

CCC Buildings Trail

Several impressive historic buildings constructed by the Depression-era Civilian Conservation Corps await day hikers in the state park.

The 0.9-mile looping CCC Buildings Trail is not an official park trail but a combination of trail segments and park roads that pass several prominent CCC structures. Among them are a "lodge," shelters, an ice house, a water tower, and a pump house.

More than 80 handcrafted stone buildings, structures and objects – all built between 1934 and 1941 – can be found at Gooseberry Falls. Known architecturally as the CCC/Rustic Style, the Minnesota Historical Society notes that "This stonework is the most visually distinctive masonry construction in the state park system." Italian stonemasons supervised the work.

The CCC consisted of unemployed young men who worked on several improvement projects across the nation during the Great Depression. Each man was paid $30 per month, much of which was sent back home to help their families.

To reach the trailhead, from Hwy. 61 turn into the park at its rest area/visitor center. Rather than park at the lots here, continue south on the entry road to the picnic area parking lot near the campgrounds.

From the lot's east side, take the middle footpath to the campground, walking down the road between campsites 62 and 63. At the next road intersection, go right/west, following the pavement.

A parking lot is on the west side; across from it, take the footpath on the road's east side to the first CCC structure, the **Campground Shelter**. Built in 1937-38, the Campground Shelter originally was a combination laundry and utility room. It since has been converted to a shelter.

Return to the campground road, then go right/northwest. After passing the next two roads leading to campsites, take the footpath going left/west to the **Ice House**. Among the last buildings constructed in 1940-41, the Ice House once was an important part of the camping trip but with modern gear and refrigeration is obsolete.

Upon returning to the campground road, go left/north. At the second road intersection, go left/west onto it. Follow it around to near Campsite 17. A footpath leads to the **Water Tower**. Among the first CCC structures built in the park, the stonework surrounds a 10,000-gallon tank.

Back on the campground road, head left/northeast. Take the next foot trail left/north to the **Lady Slipper Lodge**. Containing a fireplace and benches, the shelter gives the feeling of a true Northwoods cabin. It was the first building that the CCC erected, in 1935, as a kitchen shelter.

Continue to the other side of the shelter and pick up the park entry road. Go right/southeast onto it. Then take the footpath running left/northeast to the **Lake View Shelter**. Sitting on a hill overlooking Lake Superior, the log and stone building opened in 1936. It has picnic tables and modern restrooms.

Directly northeast of the shelter is the **Pump House**. Built in 1940, the campground used it to draw water from Lake Superior.

Looking across the Gooseberry River, you should be able to spot the **Lookout Shelter**. Opening in 1936, it can be seen up close on via the Gitchi Gummi Trail.

From the Pump House, retrace your steps back to the Lake View Shelter. A footpath runs southwest back to the parking lot where you began.

There are several other CCC structures in the park that are worth seeing. Most notable among them is the **Castle in the Park**, a retaining wall that can be seen via the Gitchi-Gami State Trail described in this volume; the CCC Worker statue on the Gateway Plaza atop the retaining wall pays homage to those who built those who served here. A **trail shelter** is on the Gitchi Gummi Trail, which includes a switchback staircase. The **Falls View Shelter** can be seen on the Nelsens Creek Trail near Upper Falls.

Gitchi-Gami State Trail

Day hikers can enjoy a quiet walk through the woods and learn about the area's geology and history on a segment of Gitchi-Gami State Trail.

Primarily a bicycle trail, the paved route can be hiked as well. When completed, the trail will run 88-miles from Two Harbors to Grand Marais. A 2.5-mile section is open in Gooseberry Falls, though, and a 4-mile round trip section of the trail makes for a great day hike.

To reach the trailhead, upon entering the state park from Hwy. 61, stay right on the park road, driving to the lower level parking lot at the campground. The trailhead is on the lot's east-central side.

From there, the trail curves southwest, heading through a quiet, largely wooded area, though with the path's width you'll still need a sunhat or sunscreen. In about 1.2 miles, it turns northeast, crossing the park entry road.

The trail next passes the Gateway Plaza, which is worth a stop. Sitting atop a 300-foot long retaining wall, known as the Castle in the Park," the plaza includes interpretive signs about the park's geology and history. The retaining wall is the Civilian Conservation Corps' largest building project in Minnesota.

From the plaza, the Gitchi-Gami cross the Gooseberry River with a view of Middle and Lower Falls downstream. The trail then parallels Hwy. 61 northeast through the rest of the park.

At two miles from the parking lot, the trail crosses Nelsens Creek. Flowing out of the hills overlooking Lake Superior, the creek's shoreline support a colorful array of wildflowers.

The creek marks a good spot to turn back. Alternately, you can continue on; Beaver Bay is a little more than 14 miles away.

Gitchi Gummi Trail

Historic buildings and views of Lake Superior from 100-foot cliffs await day hikers on the Gitchi Gummi Trail.

The trail marks a good route for getting away from the crowds at this popular park. The 2-miles round trip lollipop trail is mostly level, too.

Don't confuse this route, though, with the Gitchi-Gami Trail, which is a bicycle path that can be hiked. The Gitchi Gummi is strictly a walking trail. Its name comes from Longfellow's poem "Song of Hiawatha," which notes the shoreline of "Gitchi Gummi" (pronounced goo-me).

To reach the trailhead, use the parking lot for the waterfalls. From there, hike to the visitor center, which is a good place to stop for picking up water and taking a bathroom break before heading out.

Past the center, when the trail comes to a T-intersection, go left/north rather than to Middle and Lower Falls. You'll still get a great view of Middle Falls along the walk.

Next, the trail heads over Gooseberry River via a platform attached to the bottom of the Hwy. 61 bridge. Once across the bridge, go right/southeast. In this area, you'll pass the junction for the Gitchi-Gami Trail; watch for signs pointing to the Gitchi Gummi Snowshoe Trail.

Heading away from the bridge, the trail is wide. You'll notice small chunks of basalt mixed in the gravel surface. The weathered volcanic rock has been here for 1.1 billion years.

Growing out of this are a variety of trees common to the North Shore – spruce, paper birch, young aspen, and a few white pine. A number of wildflowers – blue bead lily, bunchberry, Canadian mayflower,   dewberry, starflower, and wood anemones – bloom here each spring.

In 0.4 miles from the trailhead, you'll reach the actual

loop. The Civilian Conservation Corps erected the stone walls here that mark the loop's start. During the Great Depression, the CCC built most of the trails and buildings seen in the park today. At the loop's start, continue straight/east so that you walk the trail counterclockwise.

As approaching Lake Superior, you'll notice larger chunks of basalt along the trail. This part of the route is on a south-facing slope, which in spring and fall receives more sunshine than those facing the other three compass directions, meaning more freeze-thaw cycles. This process, known as frost wedging, causes exposed rock to break off more quickly, resulting in chunks appropriately known as kibbles and bits.

Good views of the Gooseberry River and its estuary can be found in this section of the trail. Red and white pines dominate.

Part of the trail here also consists of planks over a grassy area that can grow swampy. Birch, spruce and pines favor this wetter section; in mid-summer, blooming wild roses along the trail fills the air with a sweet fragrance.

Full views of the lake come into sight at 0.8 miles in, as you reach a stone shelter, also built by the CCC. There are good vistas of the sand gravel bar at the river's mouth with Agate Beach on the opposite shoreline. A small spur leads to a wood outhouse, which allegedly is the only CCC-built outhouse that still stands.

Taking the stone steps leads to overlooks atop 100-foot cliffs that line the lake here. Don't get too close to the edge or take what appears to be descending paths that really are eroded portions of the cliff; instead, stick to the safe viewing platforms. Mountain ash is common here, through birch appears with greater frequency as the trail turns northeast.

Head downhill to a planked bridge and cross a creek. Marsh marigolds bloom in the wet area during spring. The trail turns north there; note how birch trees grow in size.

As the trail veers away from the lake, you'll come along-side Nelsens Creek. A small cascades on it provides a wonderfully peaceful murmur.

You'll also notice massive stumps. Most of these are of white pines that were logged off here more than a century ago.

Along the way, the loop passes eight-foot high fences that are enclosures meant to keep whitetail deer from eating tree saplings. Among the protected trees are balsam poplar, hemlock, mountain maples, paper birch and white pine.

Upon reaching a wooden shelter surrounded by birch and spruce, you've almost completed the loop. At the next trail junction, go right/northwest and retrace your steps back to the visitor center and parking lot.

Fifth Falls Trail

Day hikers can enjoy a riverside walk to a little seen waterfalls on the Fifth Falls Trail.

Though not as high or as wide as the other Upper and Middle falls, Fifth Falls is still impressive, especially during autumn. The looping trail runs 2.4–miles round trip.

Start at the park's main parking lot and walk northeast past the visitor center. At the first T-intersection, go left/north toward Upper Falls. Along the way, watch for and follow signs pointing to the Fifth Falls Snowshoe Trail.

At the Hwy. 61 bridge over the Gooseberry River, continue north along the waterway's west bank past Upper Falls. This waterfalls is about 0.2 miles from the trailhead.

After passing Upper Falls, the crowd thins considerably. Most park visitors stick to the lower three falls clustered near the visitor center, but there's plenty to see on the way to Fifth Falls.

Gooseberry River's west side definitely is the rougher of the two banks. After crossing a floodplain, the trail climbs up a steep bank. The upside: A lot of ledges along the river-bank prove fun to explore, especially for any kids accom-panying you.

After passing a horseshoe bend north of Upper Falls, the trail comes to a bridge crossing the river. Stepping onto the bridge offers good views. Once taking in the sights, stay on the river's west bank continuing straight/south.

Following a smaller horseshoe bend, the river and trail head primarily north to northwest. You'll pass a tiny water-falls, the fourth on the river (Of the Gooseberry River's five waterfalls, this hike skips Lower and Middle Falls, the two closest to Lake Superior).

At the junction with the Superior Hiking Trail, go right/ east. This takes you to a bridge over the river, about 1.1 miles from the trailhead, and delivers a great view of Fifth Falls, which is upstream.

With a 15-foot drop over ancient volcanic rock, Fifth Falls is most impressive in spring when water levels are higher from the snow melt. Autumn offers a chance to see more of the rock formations and potholes, however. You can contin-ue north past the bridge to the falls and explore the rocks up close, but be careful of any wet stones, which can be slip-pery.

Once across the bridge to the Gooseberry River's east bank, turn right/south/east. This takes you down the river, as it makes its way toward Lake Superior. This part of the route, which is shared with the Superior Hiking Trail, is wider and generally better maintained than what you walk-ed up on the opposite shore. It also offers another view of both the river's fourth waterfalls and Upper Falls.

At the Hwy. 61 bridge, which is 2.2 miles from the trailhead, take the walkway back to the Gooseberry River's east shore. Retrace your steps to the visitor center and parking lot.

Gooseberry River Trail

Day hikers can discover the berries that the park's major waterway is named for on the Gooseberry River Trail.

The 3.9–mile round trip trail heads deep into the state park's northwest corner (The Gooseberry River Trail is not the official name of trail but is used here for convenience's sake.). While you won't be out of sight of other people on the first leg of the hike, after a quarter of the way through, you'll largely walk in solitude except for songbirds and the gurgling river.

From the main parking lot for the visitor center, walk northeast past the visitor center. At the first T-intersection, go left/north toward Upper Falls. Cross the bridge over the Gooseberry River and continue north along the waterway's east bank past Upper Falls.

This part of the route, which is shared with the Superior Hiking Trail, is wider and generally better maintained than the route on the opposite shore. It offers views of both Upper Falls and the river's fourth waterfalls.

Where the Superior Hiking Trail heads west across the river, go briefly onto the bridge for a view of Fifth Falls.

Return to the trail on the river's east bank and head northwest along the river. In 0.5 miles, you'll reach a trail junction. Go left/northwest to continue along the river.

Upstream of Fifth Falls, the river flows over gravel that was left here about 10,000 years ago at the end of the last ice age. This glacial till is being washed out of the highlands into Lake Superior. The river water comes almost entirely from runoff, so its flow will be heaviest in spring as snow melts.

Along the shorelines, look for gooseberry shrubs, which prefer moist, uphill locations. They have pale green, leaves and thorn-covered stems and grow up to five feet high. Their round berry grows red and when ripe – usually in July and August – turns burgundy.

In a little more than a half-mile from the junction, the trail loops inland, away from the river. About 0.2 miles later, it reaches another trail intersection; go right/south. You gradually will head downhill. In about a half-mile, the trail reaches the junction just above Fifth Falls; go left/southeast and retrace your steps back to the parking lot.

Superior Hiking Trail

A waterfall, rugged river country, and great vistas of Lake Superior await day hikers on two segments of the Superior Hiking Trail in the state park.

The highly acclaimed SHT runs 310 miles from near Jay Cooke State Park along the North Shore to the Canadian border. In Gooseberry Falls State Park, it stays north of Hwy. 61, connecting the corner of the park's backcountry while dipping close to the main area where the waterfalls are clustered.

There's no parking lot off the Superior Hiking Trail in the state park, so you'll need to take a spur trail from the visitor center to reach it. From Hwy. 61, turn southeast into the rest area/visitor center parking for the state park. Take the paved trail heading north to the visitor center then from there watch for the signs pointing you to the Gateway Plaza. Cross under Hwy. 61 and take the footbridge over the Gooseberry River below Upper Falls. At the first trail junction, turn left/north.

In 0.34 miles, you'll find yourself the intersection with the

SHT alongside the Gooseberry River just above Upper Falls. As the waterway splits the park in half, this puts you at about the center of the SHT's run through the park.

West segment

Going left/north takes you up the Gooseberry River through the park's northwest corner. Among the highlights are a waterfalls and rugged river country in a 4.2-mile round trip.

The first section of the trail shares duty with a part of the park's Fifth Falls Trail, reaching that waterfall in 1.1 miles from the parking lot. Though only a 15-foot drop, Fifth Falls offers dramatic scenery and – unlike the popular waterfalls downriver – solitude.

Take the footbridge across the Gooseberry River above Fifth Falls. The trail then climbs away from the river shore. At the next trail junction, head right/northwest.

The trail continues to parallel the river but now is on its southwest side. In this segment, you'll notice a large 10-foot high fence that keeps whitetail deer away from the young trees on the other side. Deer love the sapling's shoots and would kill them by overgrazing.

Next, the trail heads downhill. The route becomes wide and grassy here.

The river meanders in this section. The gravel bars are excellent spots to search for agates. In spring and autumn, watch for migrating birds who stop off along here for a meal or to rest.

Where Skunk Creek joins the Gooseberry River, there's a shelter. This is about 2.1 miles from the trailhead and marks a good spot to turn back.

If you continue on, the trail then veers southwest as it follows the river and ultimately exits the park. From there, the trail heads for about seven miles to Lake County Road 103.

East segment

Alternately, at the junction above Upper Falls, you can go right/southeast, which takes you up the Gooseberry River through the park's northwest corner. Among the highlights are fantastic views of Lake Superior and the crossing of a backwoods creek in a 1.4-mile round trip hike.

The trail heads uphill through a birch and pine forest into the bluffs. This segment of the trail curves behind a knoll that blocks any views of Lake Superior, though.

The first waypoint is Nelsens Creek, which is 0.7 miles from the parking lot. The stream flows out of the highlands to the northwest into Lake Superior.

Take the footbridge over the creek. A small trail that runs directly east of the bridge leads to a great vista of the lake in 0.35 miles (one-way). That vista also marks a good spot to turn back.

The main trail does continue on into the forests above Lake Superior. Upon reaching the state park boundary, the trail heads 7.5 miles to Split Rock Lighthouse.

Nelsens Creek Trail

Day hikers can enjoy a variety of wildflowers as walking alongside a pleasant stream flowing into Lake Superior.

The Nelsens Creek Trail is not the official name of the route described here but merely a name assigned for convenience sake, as the 3.6-mile round-trip consists of segments of other trails, including cross-country ski routes.

To reach the trailhead, park in the same lot as for the River View Trail. Head past the visitor center, but rather than take the trail to Middle and Lower Falls, go left toward Upper Falls. Cross the Gooseberry River via the suspended walkway.

An asphalt pathway then passes the park's original visitor center. The material used to build the center is representative of the North Shore's geology. The black gabbro rock came from a quarry at Beaver Bay to the north, the red granite from a quarry in Duluth to the south, and the clay and sand for the mortar from Flood Bay near Two Harbors. The roof consists of cedar shakes.

The path in short order joins the Superior Hiking Trail. Go straight/northeast onto the SHT.

It's an uphill walk from here. Fortunately, the trail is wide and grassy – and also quite beautiful. The path skirts a hill composed of 1.1-billion year-old volcanic rock as heading through a forest of paper birch. During spring and summer, a variety of wildflowers bloom on this section, including Canadian mayflowers, dewberry, Mertensia, trilliums, and wood anemones.

In about a quarter mile from the old visitor center, the trail separates from the SHT upon reaching Nelsens Creek. Go left/northwest alongside the stream.

As the trail passes along the wetter and cooler stream, the wildflowers here change as well. While wood anemones are a constant, there now also are blue flag iris, coltsfoot, goldenrod, marsh marigolds, violets (both yellow and purple), and white asters. The dominant birch tree also begins to give way to spruce and aspen.

The trail soon veers northeast and crosses the creek via a footbridge. It continues uphill along the stream's east side. Look for wild rose bushes and strawberries.

Upon reaching an intersecting ski trail, continue straight/north next to the creek. Note how the dominant tree species change with aspen and spruce displacing cedar and poplar as you gain in elevation. Nelsens Creek begins at about 900 feet elevation, dropping almost 300 feet before flowing into Lake Superior.

At about 860 feet elevation, the trail veers west and crosses the creek again. Consider walking just a little beyond the footbridge; in about a tenth of a mile, the trail surface turns to red clay and pebbles, remnants of what once was Glacial Lake Duluth, the precursor to Lake Superior that around 9000 BC filled the entire valley below this point with cold meltwater.

Once you've spotted the red clay, turn back and retrace your steps to the parking lot.

Be aware that much of the trail is grassy; parts of it can be wet and even muddy in spring or after a rain, so be sure to wear good hiking boots. Also, different sources, including official park documents, provide alternate spellings for the creek, such as Nelsons, Nelson's and Nelsen's. The spelling used in this book is what appears on U.S. Geological Survey maps.

High Point Trail

Day hikers can head to the state park's highest point on the aptly named High Point Trail.

The 2.9-miles round trip trail rambles into the highlands overlooking Lake Superior after passing a number of the park's top sights, including two waterfalls and Nelsens Creek. Note that the name given to the trail here is not official but provided for easy reference.

Start by leaving your vehicle at the rest area or visitor center lots. From the parking lot, head north past the visitor center. At the first fork in the paved path, go left/northeast. The next junction overlooks Middle Falls; go left/northwest there and cross the walking bridge over the Gooseberry River at Hwy. 61. Head under the highway and pass Upper Falls along the river.

Upon reaching the Superior Hiking Trail, go right/south. The crowds thin considerably at this point, as few day hikers venture this far, and when they do, they're usually going in the opposite direction on the SHT to Fifth Falls.

The trail next swerves around the backside of a hill summit, which rises to about 880 feet. At that hill's northeast corner, you'll come to another trail junction. Stay on the Superior Hiking Trail and cross Nelsens Creek.

On the creek's other side, leave the Superior Hiking Trail by going right/southeast. At the very next trail junction, go left/northeast.

The trail is fairly flat at first but upon making a U, it climbs in elevation. As gaining in elevation throughout the trail, you'll notice that a variety of trees make up the heavy forested area. Aspen, birch, cedar and white pine dominate the highlands in the North Shore's southern part.

At the next trail junction, go left/right. This will take you to an overlook with a trail shelter. The elevation here is just a little over 900 feet, or about 300 feet above Lake Superior.

Upon taking in the view, retrace your steps back to the parking lot.

Nearby Trails

With Gooseberry Falls State Park tucked between Lake Superior and the highlands overlooking the Great Lake, the majority of day hiking trails follow the narrow strip that Minn. Hwy. 61 occupies. As the land juts into the lake and the Superior Hiking Trail traverses the bluffs and valleys cutting into them, that offers plenty of diverse hiking opportunities, from beaches to vistas, from small waterfalls to placid rivers. The best way to locate the trails is to think of how they can be reached from Hwy. 61 as either heading southwest to Two Harbors or northeast to Split Rock Lighthouse State Park.

Southwest of Gooseberry Falls

While Gooseberry Falls State Park offers plenty of trails to explore for more than a few days, there are a number of great sights nearby that bear visiting. The majority of them stretch between Two Harbors and the state park. Among the highlights are inspiring vistas of Lake Superior, agate-laden beaches, and modern harbors. The trails listed here generally run southwest from the state park to Two Harbors.

Superior Hiking Trail, Wolf Rock segment

Day hikers can enjoy impressive views of Lake Superior on the Wolf Rock segment of the Superior Hiking Trail.

The segment runs 1-mile round trip. It generally is considered one of the Superior Hiking Trail's most visually dramatic sections.

To reach the trailhead, from Gooseberry Falls State Park, head south on Hwy. 61 for about nine miles. Turn right/northwest onto Lake County Hwy. 106/W. Castle Danger Road (The highway becomes Silver Creek Township Road along the way.). In 2.3 miles is the Castle Danger Trailhead parking lot for the Superior Hiking Trail on the right/north. Take the trail heading east from the lot.

The terrain with its pines, rocky outcroppings and steepness gives you a Rocky Mountain feel. In fact, "steep" might be a kind word, as the trail gains more than 200 feet elevation in a mere half-mile.

The effort is worth it. At the top, you're rewarded with a fantastic view of the surrounding countryside, blue Lake Superior to the east and south (which is some 600 feet below), and Crow Creek to the south and west.

The summit is made of diabase, an erosion-resistant stone that has survived more than a billion years. It formed when lava flowed into fractured rock and is similar in makeup to basalt.

The summit is so named because the trail builders heard wolf howls while camping near it.

If you have a little more energy, you can continue north along the ridgeline. Going another 0.6 miles (one-way) heads through a cedar grove to a spur trail that in a mere 215 yards offers an incredible overlook of Crow Creek below.

Superior Hiking Trail, Camp Creek to Encampment River segment

Day hikers can stroll through fragrant evergreen forests between two North Shore waterways on the Superior Hiking Trail.

The 4.5-mile round trip trail connects Crow Creek and the Encampment River south of the state park.

To reach the trailhead, from Gooseberry Falls State Park, head south on Hwy. 61 for about nine miles. Turn right/ northwest onto Lake County Hwy. 106/W. Castle Danger Road (The highway becomes Silver Creek Township Road along the way.). In 2.3 miles is the Castle Danger Trailhead parking lot for the Superior Hiking Trail on the right/north. Take the trail heading west from the lot and cross Hwy. 106.

Head downhill through birches then over a talus slope (watch for signs pointing out with poison ivy to avoid). In short order, you'll arrive at Crow Creek, which sits in a deep, basalt gorge. Pause on the footbridge over the creek and examine the rock gorge, where successive lava flows from a billion years ago can be made out.

The Crow is nicknamed "Prohibition Creek" because sometimes it appears "dry." It's not an intermittent stream, though – there's just so much gravel in the creek bed that late in the summer and during autumn the water flows *be-*

neath the rocks.

For the next mile, the trail gains elevation, including a flight up wooden steps, to the top of a bluff, where a mixed maple forest stands. At the top, watch for an outcrop of rock, framed by red pines, overlooking the Crow Valley.

During the next half-mile, the trail winds to and from the bluff's edge through stands of white and red pine with dwarfed spruces and mossy-covered ground in the under-story. Mature red pine typically is 60-80 feet high, but long-lived trees can soar to 10 stories with a diameter of up to 40 inches. White pines grow slightly higher, usually between 80-100 feet with a diameter of 42 inches; the bottom of their trunk often is bare of branches.

The trail next descends through white pines to the En-campment River, offering great views along the way of the river valley inland. Many of the white pines here are around 200 years old, having survived the lumberjack era of the late 1800s.

A century ago, the Encampment River was a point of great controversy as two ideas competed over its use – one called for placing seven hydroelectric dams on it to supply Two Harbors with power while another plan called for making it a state park. Neither plan came to be.

Depending on the amount of rain, you may not be able to take the footbridge over the Encampment River. It some-times is flooded, so this marks a good spot to turn back.

Silver Creek Cliff Wayside Trail
Silver Creek Cliff Wayside/Gitchi-Gami State Trail

Day hikers can enjoy views of a massive volcanic cliff and of Lake Superior on the Silver Creek Cliff Wayside Trail.

A segment of the Gitchi-Gami State Trail, the hike runs about 0.6-miles round trip. It's paved and wide the entire way with a gradual slope upward for the first half of the walk.

To reach the trailhead, from Gooseberry Falls State Park, travel south on Hwy. 61. After passing through the Silver Creek Tunnel, turn right into the Silver Creek Cliff Wayside. The trail heads southwest from the wayside's parking lot.

To the trail's right/west is Silver Creek Cliff, which at 398 feet is the highest bluff rising out of Lake Superior. It's an awesome sight. Dark rock called diabase formed when lava flowed through this area about 1.1 billion years ago. As new lava layered itself over the older and lower flows, the trapped magma cooled slowly, forming five-sided columns. The cliff's flows sit at a 20 degree angle, typical of the rock formations surrounding Lake Superior.

A century ago, the first roads to appear in the area simply avoided this cliff by veering inland. By 1925, though, part of the cliff was cut away, and the road ran atop a sheer dropoff. With accidents due to deer that liked to stand in the middle of the road and rainstorms that often washed out the highway, a 1400-foot tunnel finally was blasted through the volcanic rock. The old road since has been converted to a biking and walking trail.

As the trail passes the tunnel entrance and climbs above it, the noise from Hwy. 61 quiets, and the impressive vista of blue Lake Superior dominates. The trail's peak is the Silver Creek Cliff Overlook.

The hike can be extended by continuing down the cliff to Old Hwy. 61/Silver Creek Road. This adds 0.4-miles roundtrip (and an uphill climb) to the hike.

Kelsey Beach Trail

Day hikers can enjoy a brief walk along one of the North Shore's best kept secrets at Kelsey Beach.

Less than a couple of hundred feet in distance, the cobblestone beach sits at the mouth of the Stewart River, as it flows into Lake Superior.

To reach the trailhead, from Gooseberry Falls State Park, take Hwy. 61 south for about 16 miles. Immediately past the Stewart River Bridge, turn right/southeast into the parking lot. A short, uneven path heads to the beach below the lot.

What awaits are black 1.1-billion-year-old lava formations and dark cobblestone that water rivulets cascade over. The dark stone contrasts nicely with the towering evergreens to the north and the clear blue of Lake Superior to the east.

The Stewart River runs just 4.9 miles out of the high grounds to the west. A protected trout stream, it hosts both "coaster" brook trout and salmon.

Named for pioneer settler John Stewart, the river once was used for log driving. So many trees were floated down the river that one log jam near the beach took three years to clear.

While the river shouldn't be waded, a bike lane on Hwy. 61 does allow hikers to cross the Stewart via a highway bridge and to explore the southern shoreline, which offers more beachfront.

As a beach walk, there's no marked trail.

Flood Bay Beach Trail

Day hikers can hunt for agates at Flood Bay Beach on the North Shore.

The crescent-shaped beach with a panoramic view of Lake Superior runs about 0.9-miles round trip if walking from the parking lot to one end of it then to the other end and back to the lot.

To reach Flood Bay, travel south from Gooseberry Falls State Park on Hwy. 61. About a mile north of Two Harbors, between mileposts 27 and 28, look for signs to the way-side/beach and turn right/east into the parking lot. From the lot, take any of the short paths east to the beach.

Flood Bay is a natural harbor. Ancient lava flows make up the rocky points at either end of the beach.

The majority of the pebbles on the beach are volcanic rocks. You can hunt for agates here; there are plenty of tiny ones, but for those with patience, many larger agates buried beneath the pebbles remain to be found. Look for striped rocks that are a shiny bluish-green or an orangish-red; the former occurs because of copper in the stone and the latter because of iron oxide.

There's plenty more to see on the beach than agates, though. After storms, driftwood washes up in piles onto the shore. Ducks, geese, beaver and – during spring – even otters often can be spotted here.

The bay was named for a settler who operated a steam sawmill on the beach in the 1850s.

A side note for budding geologists: The boulders edging the parking lot are not from the beach or immediate vicinity. The state placed them there as decoration.

Sonju Trail

A number of great sights await hikers – a trio of Great Lakes docks, wildlife including white-tailed deer, and a lake-side pine forest – on the Sonju Trail in Two Harbors. But perhaps the most impressive part of the trail is the rock beach overlooking Burlington Bay.

The paved bicycle and walking trail runs from Paul Van Hoven Park through Lakeview Park for about 2.4-miles round trip. The rock beach at the trail's northeastern end, however, offers a chance to sift through a variety of weath-ered stones, take in a beautiful view of Lake Superior's blue

Burlington Bay, and to quickly reach those lakeside pines.

To reach the rock beach, from Gooseberry Falls State Park drive south on Hwy. 61 to Two Harbors. Turn right/south on Park Road. Upon reaching the beach, park in the small lot on the road's left/east side. Alternate parking is available farther down the road at Lakeview Park.

As with most Lake Superior beaches, there is little sand but plenty of rocks. If lucky, you may even spot an agate.

Skunk Creek flows through the beach into the bay. Taking the sidewalk south over the streamlet to Lakeview Park allows day hikers to enjoy a walk on paved paths through a woods of extremely tall evergreens.

Be aware that on maps and in other literature this trail is referred to by several different names – including the "Sonju Lakewalk Trail," "Sonju Harbor Trail," and the "Two Harbors Lake Walk Trail."

Other interesting trails near Two Harbors include:

• **Two Harbors Breakwall** – Day hikers can head about a third of a mile (0.66-miles round trip) into Agate Bay along the breakwall. Park in the lots for Agate Bay Beach at the end of Third Street.

• **Lighthouse Point Trail** – The rugged 1-mile trail runs along a rocky coast and through a cedar grove on a point separating Agate and Burlington bays. Start at the southern end of the Agate Bay Beach parking lots and turn back upon reaching the junction with the Sonju (aka Two Harbors Lake Walk) Trail.

• **Lake County Demonstration Forest Trail** – About four miles of trails on an equal number of stacked loops can be found in the county forest. Parking and a trailhead are off of County Road 131/Drummond Grade at 2.7 miles from County Road 124/Holm Road.

• **Superior Hiking Trail, McCarthy Creek segment** – The

6.2-mile round trip trail heads through a sugar maple and a balsam fir forest. The parking lot off of County Road 261/ Rossini Road; head east to the McCarthy Creek crossing.

• **Knife River Rest Area Trail** – Day hikers can amble across billion-year-old rock along a river's edge at the Knife River Rest Area. To reach the Knife River Rest Area Trail, take Hwy. 61 south from Two Harbors. After milepost 18, exit to the left and double back to a parking area. The trail runs about 250-feet round trip.

• For more Two Harbors hikes, see this author's book, **Headin' to the Cabin: Day Hiking Trails of Northeast Minnesota**.

Northeast of Gooseberry Falls

Several great hiking trails also can be found north of Gooseberry Falls on the short stretch to Split Rock Lighthouse State Park. The sights include a beach of pink rock, trails winding through rare giant tufts of Arctic lichen, and a red rock gorge. The trails in this section are listed heading roughly northeast from Gooseberry Falls.

Gitchi-Gami State Trail – Twin Points segments

Incredible views of Lake Superior await day hikers of the Gitchi-Gami State Trail north of Gooseberry Falls State Park.

A 14.1-mile one–way segment of the trail heads northeast between Gooseberry Falls State Park and Beaver Bay. A good way to explore the lower half of that segment is by starting at the Twin Points Wayside.

To reach it, from Gooseberry Falls drive north on Hwy. 61. At mile marker 43, turn right/southwest into one of the two parking lots, which offers ample space.

South to Gooseberry Falls State Park

Heading southwest on the trail should start with a quick walk to the boat launch at the southwest parking lot's end. From the launch, you can access Twin Points Public Access Beach. The lot and beach used to be the sight of a Lake Superior resort.

The Gitchi-Gami can be picked up at the driveway entering the lots. Go left/southwest on the trail, which for 0.57 miles or so hugs the highway.

Next the trail swerves southeast to a quieter, wooded area away from the highway. When the trail curves southwest again, watch for and take one of the dirt paths heading southeast; these lead to Thompson Beach, which stretches a little under a quarter mile along Lake Superior.

About 0.5 miles after leaving Hwy. 61, the Gitchi-Gami rejoins it. That spot marks a good turnback point to head back. Alternately, you can continue walking to Gooseberry Falls State Park, whose parking lot is 1.18 miles ahead with Upper Falls along the way.

North to West Split Rock River

Alternately, from Twin Points, the trail can be hiked north to Split Rock Lighthouse State Park's West Split Rock River (a little more than 4-miles round trip).

From the northern parking lot, head right/northeast onto the wooded trail. The route immediately passes a connector trail to Iona's Beach, whose pink rock shoreline warrants a trip all on its own.

In a quarter mile from the parking lot, the trail again runs alongside Hwy. 61. About 0.3 miles later, it comes right up to Lake Superior. This narrow spot marks a good spot to turn back.

Alternately, you can continue walking northeast to Split Rock Lighthouse State Park. The Split Rock River Wayside is in about 0.9 miles.

Corundum Mine Trail

Another fascinating segment of the Gitchi-Gami State Trail north of Gooseberry Falls is the Corundum Mine Trail. Lake Superior can be enjoyed along Split Rock Point via a 1.8-mile round trip.

Park at the Hwy. 61 wayside immediately before Split Rock River; cross the highway and join the Gitchi-Gami State Trail that goes over the river. After the bridge, take the first trail heading right/southeast, then follow the connector trail overlooking Crazy Bay.

Iona's Beach Trail
Iona's Beach Scientific and Natural Area

Day hikers can stroll a beach of pink rock on the North Shore.

The stem trail and lakeshore at Iona's Beach Scientific and Natural Area run 0.7-miles round trip. You probably won't need to walk that far, though – the beach is a mere fifth of a mile from the parking lot.

To reach Iona's Beach, from Gooseberry Falls State Park drive north on Hwy. 61. At milepost 41, turn right/east into the Twin Points Boat Launch. Veer to the parking lot on the left/north for Iona's Beach.

From the wayside lot, a rustic trail heads past towering, fragrant pines with the dappled light of the sun sifting through the branches. Part of the path to the beach is shared with the Gitchi-Gami State Trail, so be careful of not continuing north on the bike trail when it splits from the route leading to the shoreline.

As closing on the beach, glimpses of Lake Superior appear through the pines.

In a mere thousand feet from the lot, the trail opens up to a scene out of a fairy tale – a beach of utterly pink rock, layered in wavy patterns as the baby blue waters of Lake Superior lap against it.

Stepping onto the beach, which stretches three football fields long, the piles of thin flat rocks crackle and crunch beneath your feet. The pink rocks come from a cliff of pink rhyolite at the beach's north end. A point of ancient basalt at the beach's south end prevents the pebbles – known by geologists as shingles – from drifting southward, allowing them to pile up here.

The pinkness can be somewhat blinding. But not every rock is that color – there are a few rare gray ones in the mix that lovers who've previously walked here have gathered and placed into the shapes of hearts that stand out against the light rose stones.

There's also a long tree log that's been bleached to the color of chalk, and sometimes a white seagull will flit past, making its *screeeee!* call.

But mostly the beach is quiet as you sit upon the log and take in the vast lake, letting all of your worries fade with horizon.

After enjoying the sights, retrace your steps back to the parking lot.

Superior Hiking Trail, Blueberry Hill Road to Split Rock River Valley segment

Dazzling vistas of Lake Superior and massive tufts of Arctic lichen await day hikers on a segment of the Superior Hiking Trail north of Gooseberry Falls State Park.

After leaving Gooseberry Falls, Minnesota's Superior Hiking Trail meanders for six miles across a ridge overlooking Lake Superior on its way to Split Rock Lighthouse State Park. This route could be treated as a point-to-point trail; another approach that is more convenient to day hikers is to split it into two sections by starting at Blueberry Hill Road.

To reach this access point, from Gooseberry Falls State Park, drive north on Minn. Hwy. 61. Turn left/northwest onto Blueberry Hill Road, whose dirt surface as it climbs into the forested hills quickly will have you feeling like you've truly entered a remote wilderness.

Watch closely for a break in the woods where the Superior Hiking Trail crosses the road. Park on the road's shoulder.

Going west toward Gooseberry Falls is peaceful as the trail

runs through birch groves along the ridge's base. Gooseberry River is 2.8 miles away from the road.

Heading east, however, offers several great vistas. The somewhat challenging path starts with an steep but short climb to the top of Bread Loaf Ridge. Spectacular views of Lake Superior and the forest below abound for about a mile.

There's also a lot of rare sites to see in the forest itself.

You'll likely notice reindeer moss, a lichen that usually is found in the polar regions. On the ridge, they form hemispherical tufts about the size of a bushel basket; when that large, the moss probably is about a century old.

There's also a lot of weathered rock. These outcroppings mark the top of a series of lava flows that 1.1 billion years ago covered this section of the continent. Exposure to wind, rain, freezing and glaciers over the eons have exposed this ancient, underlying basalt at several spots on the forest floor.

You also won't be able to help but smell the wild roses when they bloom in June through July. The sweet-scented five-petaled pink flower with its yellow center stands starkly against kelly green leaves.

At 1.6 miles from trailhead, the Superior Hiking Trail descends into the Split Rock River Valley. This marks a good spot to turn back for a 3.2-mile round trip.

Should you continue on, the trail makes a steep climb back up the other side of the valley then an easy descent through a birch grove before reaching a waterfall on a branch of the Split Rock River. The waterfall is 2.7 miles (one-way) from Blueberry Hill Road but can be more easily reached by taking the Superior Hiking Trail from the Split Rock River Wayside.

Split Rock River Trail
Split Rock Lighthouse State Park

A red rock gorge with waterfalls awaits day hikers of the Split Rock River Trail.

The 4.4-miles round trip trail sits in Split Rock Lighthouse State Park. Due to the great scenery and ease of access, it's also among the Superior Hiking Trail's most popular segments.

To reach the trail, from Gooseberry Falls State Park, drive north on Hwy. 61. At mile marker 43.2, turn into the parking lot for the Split Rock River Wayside on the road's north side.

The path heads up the west shore of Split Rock River through a birch grove on a spur trail. The spur is a gradual climb, offering nice views of the river valley below. Be aware that the clay banks on this side of the root beer-colored river at times are steep and after a rainfall can be slick; boardwalks, timbers and bridges make up part of the rugged trail's surface.

At 0.5 miles from the trailhead, the spur reaches the junction with the actual Superior Hiking Trail; go right/north, remaining along the river. Watch for the blue blazes that mark the SHT.

A wooden bridge crosses the West Fork of the Split River, a small creek that drains into the main waterway, at about 0.8 miles from the trailhead. Large, mature cedars grow near the confluence, and a rock ledge allows a great place to rest and even enjoy a picnic as viewing Split Rock Falls, which tumbles 20 feet over gray rock.

From the creek, the trail swerves back to the river and enters a magnificent red rock gorge. The rock is rhyolite, a form of granite that appears red though its crystals are pink, black and white.

It formed during a massive lava flow 1.1 billion years ago.

A bare, shear five-story cliff of rhyolite is visible on the opposite shore. The green conifers atop this wall nicely contrast with the red rock.

Cascades and a small waterfall also can be found within the gorge.

Also among the highlights is the Pillars, twin chimneys of rhyolite. They sometimes are referred to as "Split Rock," though that appellation probably came after the park was named. Passing the formation, look back as the pillars frame the waterfalls in the gorge.

Leaving the gorge, the trail levels out. At 2.4 miles, it reaches a bridge over the Split River; this marks a good spot to turn back to the parking lot.

Additional hike

If you have a little extra energy, consider making a loop around the river. Rather than turn back at the bridge, cross it to the river's east side for a 5-mile round trip.

This trail on the eastern/northern shoreline is higher, staying above the gorge. Combined with the greater amount of sunlight the slopes on this side of the river receive, this is a drier portion of the trail. The cliffs also offer a unique vantage for seeing the Pillars.

The trail soon moves away from the river and climbs a bit higher to a ridgeline. The result is a wide, commanding view of Lake Superior with the Apostle Islands in the distance. A lean-to shelter is near this vista.

At 4.2 miles from the parking lot, the Superior Hiking Trail comes to a junction; take the spur trail right/southeast. The trail then makes a steep descent. At the bottom, you'll cross Hwy. 61. From there, go left, southwest on the paved Gitchi-Gami State Trail.

The trail then crosses Split Rock as it spills into Lake Superior. Use the pedestrian tunnel to cross Hwy. 61 to your parking lot.

Split Rock Light Station Trail
Split Rock Lighthouse State Park

Day hikers can explore one of the nation's most famous lighthouses and enjoy impressive cliff top views of Lake Superior on the Split Rock Light Station Trail.

The 0.8-mile trail is a collection of walking paths around the historic Split Rock lighthouse. Perched atop a 130-foot high solid rock cliff overlooking Lake Superior, Split Rock is among the most photographed lighthouses in the country. The Minnesota Historical Society operates the 25-acre site in Split Rock Lighthouse State Park.

To reach the lighthouse from Gooseberry Falls State Park, drive north for about nine miles on Hwy. 61. Take the main park road to parking area for Split Rock Light Station and History Center.

Keeper's house

Begin the hike at the parking lot's southeast end by taking the walking path to the visitor center. After enjoying the exhibits, head back to the parking lot's southwest end and go west on the Little Two Harbors Trail.

At the second junction, head south, taking the trail downhill to the pump house and the old dock location on the lake. When the lighthouse was being constructed and for almost a quarter century after its opening, it could only be reached by water.

Initially, this required that supplies be hoisted by crane from ships to the clifftop. By 1916, though, a tramway was constructed so that supplies could be brought up in a cart, with a gasoline engine powering the cables. Today, only the tramway's concrete support piers stand.

Retrace your steps to Little Two Harbors Trail and head right/east. Take the next trail heading right/south. This passes two buildings of a private residence then the restored keeper's home on the left/north.

Summer visitors can go inside the two-story brick house (It and two other grounds buildings are open from mid-May to mid-October, usually 10 a.m. to 6 p.m.). The cozy first floor consists of a kitchen, dining room and living room while the upstairs has three bedrooms and a bath. A cistern is in the cellar.

Lighthouse, fog-signal building

Leaving the keeper's house, continue on the trail. Go right/south at the next junction to the brick fog-signal building and the lighthouse.

Visitors also can go inside the fog-signal building. When the light station opened more than a century ago, two six-inch sirens, powered by a 22-horsepower gasoline engine, warned off ships that might not be able to see the lighthouse beacon due to fog.

Next to the fog-signal building is the lighthouse, which recently was restored to its pre-1924 appearance. Summer visitors can enter the octagonal brick tower, which was built around a steel framework. The lighthouse stands 54-feet high, with a lens manufactured in France that flashed every 10 seconds. Officially, the light could be seen up to 22 miles away, but fishermen in Grand Marais, Minn., more than 60 miles away, reported they could spot it on clear nights.

Take the walking trail north from the lighthouse and past the keeper's home, as if heading to the visitor center. At the next trail junction, go right/southeast by the oil house.

As the trail reaches the cliff overlooking Lake Superior, the route curves north past the old hoist location. The hoist was used to supply the lighthouse until the tram opened, which in turn was displaced by the nearby highway.

That road wasn't constructed until 1929, and even then a driveway to the lighthouse wasn't built until 1944. Still, the road during the Great Depression began Split Rock's tourism tradition. During 1938, close to 100,000 people visited the lighthouse by parking off the road and hiking to the site. It probably was the most visited lighthouse in America during that decade, the Coast Guard reported at the time.

Lake Superior views

Following the hoist site, go straight/north at the next junction for a grand view of Lake Superior. The world's largest freshwater body of water, Lake Superior covers 31,700 square miles and reaches a depth of 1,332 feet.

After taking in the beautiful lake views, retrace your steps back to last trail junction. Once there, go right/west back to the parking lot.

The station officially closed in 1969 and in the decades since became a state park and a National Historic Landmark.

Visitors should note that while pets are allowed in the state park, they cannot go the historic area.

Other Split Rock Lighthouse State Park trails

• **Day Hill Trail** – This 1.3-miles round trip heads to a summit overlooking Lake Superior. Park at the lot at the end of Split Rock's entrance road then take the stem trail south toward the lake. At the second junction, go right/northwest and head around the base of Day Hill, following the route to the summit.

• **Merrill Logging Trail** – Day hikers can travel into the bluffs overlooking Lake Superior via a century-old railroad grade. The trail, including the access from the DOT wayside for Split Rock River, runs 2.7-miles round trip. It crosses an area that many visiting the state rock bypass in favor of the historic lighthouse.

• **Gitchi-Gami State Trail** – Take the trail north of the lighthouse to Gold Rock Point for a 4-mile round trip. On the point, you can look for agates and try to spot in the shallow water the remains of the cargo ship *Madeira*, which sunk here in 1905.

• For more hikes northeast of Split Rock Lighthouse State Park, see this author's book, **Headin' to the Cabin: Day Hiking Trails of Northeast Minnesota**.

Best Trails Lists

Which trails are the best for watching birds? To enjoy fall colors? For its great vistas? Here are some lists of the best Gooseberry Falls State Park trails for those and many other specific interests (Italicized trails are outside of the park.).

Autumn leaves
• Fifth Falls Trail
• River View Trail

Beaches
• River View Trail (for Agate Beach)
• *Flood Bay Beach Trail*
• *Iona's Beach Trail*

Birdwatching
• Gooseberry River Trail
• River View Trail
• Superior Hiking Trail, West segment

Campgrounds
• CCC Buildings Trail
• Gitchi-Gami State Trail
• Picnic Flow Trail

Geology
• Gooseberry River Trail
• *Iona's Beach Trail*

- Picnic Flow Trail
- River View Trail
- *Split Rock River Trail*

History/Archeology
- CCC Buildings Trail
- Gitchi-Gami State Trail (Gateway Plaza)
- *Split Rock Light Station Trail*

Lake Superior vistas
- Gitchi-Gummi Trail
- Picnic Flow Trail
- *Silver Creek Cliff Wayside Trail*

Must-do's
- Picnic Flow Trail
- River View Trail
- Superior Hiking Trail

Picnicking
- CCC Buildings Trail
- Picnic Flow Trail
- *Split Rock River Trail*

Plant communities
- Gooseberry River Trail
- Nelsens Creek Trail
- *Superior Hiking Trail, Blueberry Hill Road to Split Rock River Valley* segment

Waterfalls
- Fifth Falls Trail
- River View Trail
- *Split Rock River Trail*

Wildflowers
- Gitchi-Gummi Trail
- Nelsens Creek Trail
- Picnic Flow Trail

Bonus Section:
Day Hiking Primer

You'll get more out of a day hike if you research it and plan ahead. It's not enough to just pull over to the side of the road and hit a trail that you've never been on and have no idea where it goes. In fact, doing so invites disaster.

Instead, you should preselect a trail (This book's trail descriptions can help you do that). You'll also want to ensure that you have the proper clothing, equipment, navigational tools, first-aid kit, food and water. Knowing the rules of the trail and potential dangers along the way also are helpful. In this special section, we'll look at each of these topics to ensure you're fully prepared.

Selecting a Trail

For your first few hikes, stick to short, well-known trails where you're likely to encounter others. Once you get a feel for hiking, your abilities, and your interests, expand to longer and more remote trails.

Always check to see what the weather will be like on the trail you plan to hike. While an adult might be able to withstand wind and a sprinkle here or there, if you bring kids, for them it can be pure misery. Dry, pleasantly warm days with limited wind always are best when hiking with children.

Don't choose a trail that is any longer than the least fit person in your group can hike. Adults in good shape can go

8-12 miles a day; for kids, it's much less. There's no magical number.

When planning the hike, try to find a trail with a mid-point payoff – that is something you and definitely any children will find exciting about half-way through the hike. This will help keep up everyone's energy and enthusiasm during the journey.

If you have children in your hiking party, consider a couple of additional points when selecting a trail.

Until children enter their late teens, they need to stick to trails rather than going off-trail hiking, which is known as bushwhacking. Children too easily can get lost when off trail. They also can easily get scratched and cut up or stumble across poisonous plants and dangerous animals.

Generally, kids will prefer a circular route to one that requires hiking back the way you came. The return trip often feels anti-climatic, but you can overcome that by mentioning features that all of you might want to take a closer look at.

Once you select a trail, it's time to plan for your day hike. Doing so will save you a lot of grief – and potentially prevent an emergency – later on. You are, after all, entering the wilds, a place where help may not be readily available.

When planning your hike, follow these steps:

• Print a road map showing how to reach the parking lot near the trailhead. Outline the route with a transparent yellow highlighter and write out the directions.

• Print a satellite photo of the parking area and the trailhead. Mark the trailhead on the photo.

• Print a topo map of the trail. Outline the trail with the yellow highlighter. Note interesting features you want to see along the trail and the destination.

• If carrying GPS, program this information into your device.

• Make a timeline for your trip, listing: when you will leave home; when you will arrive at the trailhead; your turn back time; when you will return for home in your vehicle; and when you will arrive at your home.

• Estimate how much water and food you will need to bring based on the amount of time you plan to spend on the trail and in your vehicle. You'll want to carry at least two pints of water per person for every hour on the trail.

• Fill out two copies of a hiker's safety form. Leave one in your vehicle.

• Share all of this information with a responsible person remaining in civilization, leaving a hiker's safety form with them. If they do not hear from you within an hour of when you plan to leave the trail in your vehicle, they should contact authorities to report you as possibly lost.

Clothing
Footwear

If your feet hurt, the hike is over, so getting the right footwear is worth the time. With children, if you've gone a few weeks without hiking, that's plenty of time for feet to grow, and they may have just outgrown their hiking boots. Check out everyone's footwear a few days before heading out on the hike. If it doesn't fit, replace it.

For flat, smooth, dry trails, sneakers and cross-trainers are fine, but if you really want to head onto less traveled roads or tackle areas that aren't typically dry, you'll need hiking boots.

Once you start doing any rocky or steep trails – and remember that a trail you consider moderately steep needs to be only half that angle for a child to consider it ex-tremely steep – you'll want hiking boots, which offer rugged tread perfect for handling rough trails.

Socks

Socks serve two purposes: to wick sweat away from skin and to provide cushioning. Cotton socks aren't very good for hiking, except in extremely dry environments, because they retain moisture that can result in blisters. Wool socks or liner socks work best, so you'll want to look for three-season socks, also known as trekking socks. While a little thicker than summer socks, their extra cushioning generally prevents blisters. Also, make sure kids don't put on holey socks; that's just inviting blisters.

Layering

On all but hot, dry days, wear multiple layers of clothing that provide various levels of protection against sweat, heat loss, wind and potentially rain. Layering works because the type of clothing you select for each stratum serves a different function, such as wicking moisture or shielding against wind. In addition, trapped air between each layer of clothing is warmed by your body heat. Layers also can be added or taken off as needed.

Generally, you need three layers. Closest to your skin is the wicking layer, which pulls perspiration away from the body and into the next layer, where it evaporates. Exertion from walking means you will sweat and generate heat, even if the weather is cold. The second layer is an insulation layer, which helps keep you warm. The last layer is a water-resistant shell that protects you from rain, wind, snow and sleet.

As the seasons and weather change, so does the type of clothing you select for each layer. The first layer ought to be a loose-fitting T-shirt in summer, but in winter and on other cold days you might opt for a long-sleeved moisture-wicking synthetic material, like polypropylene. During winter, the next layer probably also should cover the neck, which often is exposed to the elements. A turtleneck works fine, but preferably not one made of cotton. The third layer in winter, depending on the temperature, could be a wool sweater, a half-zippered long sleeved fleece jacket, or a fleece vest.

You might even add a fourth layer of a hooded parka with pockets, made of material that can block wind and resist water. Gloves or mittens as well as a hat also are necessary on cold days.

Headgear

Half of all body heat is lost through the head, hence the hiker's adage, "If your hands are cold, wear a hat." In cool, wet weather, wearing a hat is at least good for avoiding hy-pothermia, a potentially deadly condition in which heat loss occurs faster than the body can generate it. Children are more susceptible to hypothermia than adults.

Especially during summer, a hat with a wide brim is useful in keeping the sun out of eyes. It's also nice should rain start to fall.

For young children, get a hat with a chin strap. They like to play with their hats, which will fly off in a wind gust if not "fastened" some way to the child.

Sunglasses

Sunglasses are an absolute must if walking through open areas exposed to the sun and in winter when you can suffer from snow blindness. Look for 100% UV-protective shades, which provide the best screen.

Equipment

A couple of principles should guide your purchases. First, the longer and more complex the hike, the more equipment you'll need. Secondly, your general goal is to go light. Since you're on a day hike, the amount of gear you'll need is a fraction of what backpackers shown in magazines and catalogues usually carry. Still, the inclination of most day hikers is to not carry enough equipment. For the lightness issue, most gear today is made with titanium and siliconized nylon, ensuring it is sturdy yet fairly light. While the following list of what you need may look long, it won't weigh much.

Backpacks

Sometimes called daypacks (for day hikes or for kids), backpacks are necessary to carry all of the essentials you need – snacks, first-aid kit, extra clothing.

For day hiking, you'll want to get yourself an internal frame, in which the frame giving the backpack its shape is inside the pack's fabric so it's not exposed to nature. Such frames usually are lightweight and comfortable. External frames have the frame outside the pack, so they are exposed to the elements. They are excellent for long hikes into the backcountry when you must carry heavy loads.

As kids get older, and especially after they've been hiking for a couple of years, they'll want a "real" backpack. Unfortunately, most backpacks for kids are overbuilt and too heavy. Even light ones that safely can hold up to 50 pounds are inane for most children.

When buying a daypack for your child, look for sternum straps, which help keep the strap on the shoulders. This is vital for prepubescent children as they do not have the broad shoulders that come with adolescence, meaning packs likely will slip off and onto their arms, making them uncomfortable and difficult to carry. Don't buy a backpack that a child will "grow into." Backpacks that don't fit well simply will lead to sore shoulder and back muscles and could result in poor posture.

Also, consider purchasing a daypack with a hydration system for kids. This will help ensure they drink a lot of water. More on this later when we get to canteens.

Before hitting the trail, always check your children's backpacks to make sure that they have not overloaded them. Kids think they need more than they really do. They also tend to overestimate their own ability to carry stuff. Sibling rivalries often lead to children packing more than they should in their rucksacks, too. Don't let them overpack "to teach them a lesson," though, as it can damage bones and turn the hike into a bad experience.

A good rule of thumb is no more than 25 percent capacity. Most upper elementary school kids can carry only about 10 pounds for any short distance. Subtract the weight of the backpack, and that means only 4-5 pounds in the backpack. Overweight children will need to carry a little less than this or they'll quickly be out of breath.

Child carriers

If your child is an infant or toddler, you'll have to carry him. Until infants can hold their heads up, which usually doesn't happen until about four to six months of age, a front pack (like a Snugli or Baby Bjorn) is best. It keeps the infant close for warmth and balances out your backpack. At the same time, though, you must watch for baby overheating in a front pack, so you'll need to remove the infant from your body at rest stops.

Once children reach about 20 pounds, they typically can hold their heads up and sit on their own. At that point, you'll want a baby carrier (sometimes called a baby backpack or a child carrier), which can transfer the infant's weight to your hips when you walk. You'll not only be comfortable, but your child will love it, too.

Look for a baby carrier that is sturdy yet lightweight. Your child is going to get heavier as time passes, so about the only way you can counteract this is to reduce the weight of the items you use to carry things. The carrier also should have adjustment points, as you don't want your child to outgrow the carrier too soon. A padded waist belt and padded shoulder straps are necessary for your comfort.

The carrier should provide head and neck support if you're hauling an infant. It also should offer back support for children of all ages, and leg holes should be wide enough so there's no chafing. You want to be able to load your infant without help, so it should be stable enough to stand that way when you take it off so the child can sit in it for a moment while you get turned around.

Stay away from baby carriers with only shoulder straps as you need the waist belt to help shift the child's weight to your hips for more comfortable walking.

Fanny packs

Also known as a belt bag, a fanny pack is virtually a must for anyone with a baby carrier as you can't otherwise lug a backpack.

If your significant other is with you, he or she can carry the backpack, of course. Still, the fanny pack also is a good alternative to a backpack in hot weather, as it will reduce back sweat.

If you have only one or two kids on a hike, or if they also are old enough to carry daypacks, your fanny pack need not be large. A mid-size pouch can carry at least 200 cubic inches of supplies, which is more than enough to accom-modate all the materials you need. A good fanny pack also has a place to hook canteens to it.

Canteens

Canteens or plastic bottles filled with water are vital for any hike, no matter how short the trail. You'll need to have enough of them to carry about two pints of water per person for every hour of hiking.

Trekking poles

Also known as walking poles or walking sticks, trekking poles are necessary for maintaining stability on uneven or wet surfaces and to help reduce fatigue. The latter makes them useful on even surfaces. By transferring weight to the arms, a trekking pole can reduce stress on knees and lower back, allowing you to maintain better posture and to go farther.

If a baby or toddler is on your back, you'll primarily want a trekking pole to help you maintain your balance, even if on a flat surface, and to help absorb some of the impact of your step.

Graphite tips provide the best traction. A basket just above the tip is a good idea so the stick doesn't sink into mud or sand. Angled cork handles are ergonomic and help absorb sweat from your hands so they don't blister. A strap on the handle to wrap around your hand is useful so the stick doesn't slip out. Telescopic poles are a good idea as you can adjust them as needed based on the terrain you're hiking and as kids grow to accommodate their height.

The pole also needs to be sturdy enough to handle rugged terrain, as you don't want one that bends when you press it to the ground.

Spring-loaded shock absorbers help when heading down a steep incline but aren't necessary. Indeed, for a short walk across flat terrain, the right length stick is about all you need.

Carabiners

Carabiners are metal loops, vaguely shaped like a D, with a sprung or screwed gate. You'll find that hooking a couple of them to your backpack or fanny pack useful in many ways. For example, if you need to dig through a fanny pack, you can hook the strap of your trekking pole to it. Your hat, camera straps, first-aid kit, and a number of other objects also can connect to them. Hook carabiners to your fanny pack or backpack upon purchasing them so you don't forget them when packing. Small carabiners with sprung gates are inexpensive, but they do have a limited life span of a couple of dozen hikes.

Navigational Tools

Paper maps

Paper maps may sound passé in this age of GPS, but you'll find the variety and breadth of view they offer to be useful. During the planning process, a paper map (even if viewing it online), will be far superior to a GPS device. On the hike, you'll also want a backup to GPS. Or like many casual hikers, you may not own GPS at all, which makes paper maps indispensable.

Standard road maps (which includes printed guides and handmade trail maps) show highways and locations of cities and parks. Maps included in guidebooks, printed guides handed out at parks, and those that are hand-drawn tend to be designed like road maps, and often carry the same positives and negatives.

Topographical maps give contour lines and other important details for crossing a landscape. You'll find them invaluable on a hike into the wilds. The contour lines' shape and their spacing show the form and steepness of a hill or bluff, unlike the standard road map and most brochures and hand-drawn trail maps. You'll also know if you're in a woods, which is marked in green, or in a clearing, which is marked in white. If you get lost, figuring out where you are and how to get to where you need to be will be much easier with such information.

Satellite photos offer a view from above that is rendered exactly as it would look from an airplane. Thanks to Google and other online services, you can get fairly detailed pictures of the landscape. Such pictures are an excellent resource when researching a hiking trail. Unfortunately, those pictures don't label what a feature is or what it's called, as would a topo map. Unless there's a stream, determining if a feature is a valley bottom or a ridgeline also can be difficult. Like topo maps, satellite photos can be out of date a few years.

GPS

By using satellites, the global positioning system can find your spot on the Earth to within 10 feet. Aa GPS device allows you to preprogram the trailhead location and mark key turns and landmarks as well as the hike's endpoint. This mobile map is a powerful technological tool that almost certainly ensures you won't get lost – so long as you've correctly programmed the information. GPS also can calculate travel time and act as a compass, a barometer and altimeter, making such devices seemingly obsolete on a hike.

Still, in remote areas, reception is spotty at best for GPS, rendering your mobile map worthless. A GPS device also runs on batteries, and there's always a chance they will go dead. Or you may drop your device, breaking it in the process. Their screens are small, and sometimes you need a large paper map to get a good sense of the natural landmarks around you.

Compass

Like a paper map, a compass is indispensable even if you use GPS. Should your GPS no longer function, the compass then can be used to tell you which direction you're heading. A protractor compass is best for hiking. Beneath the compass needle is a transparent base with lines to help you orient yourself. The compass often serves as a magnifying glass to help you make out map details. Most protractor compasses also come with a lanyard for easy carrying.

Food and Water

Water

As water is the heaviest item you'll probably carry, there is a temptation to not take as much as one should. Don't skimp on the amount of water you bring, though; after all, it's the one supply your body most needs. It's always better to end up having more water than you needed than returning to your vehicle dehydrated.

Adults need at least a quart for every two hours hiking. Children need to drink about a quart every two hours of walking and more if the weather is hot or dry. To keep kids hydrated, have them drink at every rest stop.

Don't presume there will be water on the hiking trail. Most trails outside of urban areas lack such amenities. In addition, don't drink water from local streams, lakes, rivers or ponds. There's no way to tell if local water is safe or not. As soon as you've consumed half of your water supply, you should turn around for the vehicle.

Food

Among the many wonderful things about hiking is that snacking between meals isn't frowned upon. You want to keep everyone in your hiking party fed, especially as hunger can lead to lethargic and discontented children. It'll also keep toddlers from snacking on flora or dirt. Before hitting the trail, re-package as much of the food as possible, as products sold at grocery stores tend to come in bulky packages that take up space and add a little weight to your backpack. Instead, place the food in re-sealable plastic bags.

Bring a variety of small snacks for rest stops. You don't want kids filling up on snacks, but you do need them to maintain their energy levels if they're walking or to ensure they don't turn fussy if riding in a baby carrier. Go for complex carbohydrates and proteins for maintaining energy. Good options include dried fruits, jerky, nuts, peanut butter, prepared energy bars, candy bars with a high protein content (nuts, peanut butter), crackers, raisins and trail mix (called "gorp"). A number of trail mix recipes are available online; you and your children may want to try them out at home to see which ones you collectively like most.

Salty treats rehydrate better than sweet treats do. Chocolate and other sweets are fine if they're not all that's exclusively served, but remember they also tend to lead to thirst and to make sticky messes. Whichever snacks you choose, if with children don't experiment with food on the trail. Bring what you know the kids will like.

Give the first snack within a half-hour of leaving the trailhead or you risk children becoming tired and whiny from low energy levels. If kids start asking for them every few steps, even after having something to eat at the last rest stop, consider timing snacks to reaching a seeable landmark, such as, "We'll get out the trail mix when we reach that bend up ahead."

What not to bring

Avoid soda and other caffeinated beverages, alcohol, and

energy pills. The caffeine will dehydrate children as well as you. Alcohol has no place on the trail; you need your full faculties when making decisions and driving home. Energy pills essentially are a stimulant and like alcohol can lead to bad calls. If you're tired, get some sleep and hit the trail another day.

First-aid Kit

After water, this is the most essential item you can carry. A first-aid kit should include:

• Adhesive bandages of various types and sizes, especially butterfly bandages (for younger kids, make sure they're colorful kid bandages)

• Aloe vera

• Anesthetic (such as Benzocaine)

• Antacid (tablets)

• Antibacterial (aka antibiotic) ointment (such as Neosporin or Bacitracin)

• Anti-diarrheal tablets (for adults only, as giving this to a child is controversial)

• Anti-itch cream or calamine lotion

• Antiseptics (such as hydrogen peroxide, iodine or Betadine, Mercuroclear, rubbing alcohol)

• Baking soda

• Breakable (or instant) ice packs

• Cotton swabs

• Disposable syringe (w/o needle)

• Epipen (if children or adults have allergies)

• Fingernail clippers (your multi-purpose tool might have this, and if so you can dispense with it)

• Gauze bandage

• Gauze compress pads (2x2 individually wrapped pad)

• Hand sanitizer (use this in place of soap)

• Liquid antihistamine (not Benadryl tablets, however, as children should take liquid not pills; be aware that liquid antihistamines may cause drowsiness)
  • Medical tape
  • Moisturizer containing an anti-inflammatory
  • Mole skin
  • Pain reliever (a.k.a. aspirin; for children's pain relief, use liquid acetaminophen such Tylenol or liquid ibuprofen; never give aspirin to a child under 12)
  • Poison ivy cream (for treatment)
  • Poison ivy soap
  • Powdered sports drinks mix or electrolyte additives
  • Sling
  • Snakebite kit
  • Thermometer
  • Tweezers (your multi-purpose tool may have this allowing you to dispense with it)
  • Water purification tablets

If infants and toddlers are with you, be sure to also carry teething ointment (such as Orajel) and diaper rash treatment.

Many of the items should be taken out of their store packaging to make placement in your fanny pack or backpack easier. In addition, small amounts of some items – such as baking soda and cotton swabs – can be placed inside re-sealable plastic bags, since you won't need the whole purchased amount.

Make sure the first-aid items are in a waterproof container. A re-sealable plastic zipper bag is perfectly fine. In humid climates, be sure to replace the adhesive bandages every couple of months, as they can deteriorate in the moistness. Also, check your first-aid kit every few trips and after any hike in which you've just used it, so that you can replace what's been used and to ensure medicines haven't expired.

If you have older elementary-age kids and teenagers who've been trained in first aid, giving them a kit to carry as well as yourself is a good idea. Should they find themselves lost or if you cannot get to them for a few moments, the kids might need to provide very basic first aid to one another.

Hiking with Children: Attitude Adjustment

To enjoy hiking with kids, you'll first have to adopt your child's perspective. Simply put, we must learn to hike on our kids' schedules.

Compared to adults, kids can't walk as far, they can't walk as fast, and they will grow bored more quickly. Every step we take requires three for them. In addition, early walkers, up to two years of age, prefer to wander than to "hike." Pre-school kids will start to walk the trail, but at a rate of only about a mile per hour. With stops, that can turn a three-mile hike into a four-hour journey. Kids also won't be able to hike as steep of trails as you or handle as inclement of weather as you might.

This all may sound limiting, especially to long-time back-packers used to racking up miles or bagging peaks on their hikes, but it's really not. While you may have to put off some backcountry and mountain climbing trips for a while, it also opens up to you a number of great short trails and nature hikes with spectacular sights that you may have otherwise skipped because they weren't challenging enough.

So sure, you'll have to make some compromises, but the payout is high. You're not personally on the hike to get a workout but to spend quality time with your children.

Family Dog

Dogs are part of the family, and if you have children,

they'll want to share the hiking experience with their pets. In turn, dogs will have a blast on the trail, some larger dogs can be used as Sherpas, and others will defend against threatening animals.

But there is a downside to dogs. Many will chase animals and so run the risk of getting lost or injured. Also, a doggy bag will have to be carried for dog pooh – yeah, it's natural, but also inconsiderate to leave for other hikers to smell and for their kids to step in. In addition, most dogs almost always will lose a battle against a threatening animal, so there's a price to be paid for your safety.

Many places where you'll hike solve the dilemma for you as dogs aren't allowed on their trails. Dogs are verboten on some state park trails but usually permitted on those in national forests. Always check with the park ranger before heading to the trail.

If you can bring a dog, make sure it is well behaved and friendly to others. You don't need your dog biting another hiker while unnecessarily defending its family.

Rules of the Trail

Ah, the woods or a wide open meadow, peaceful and quiet, not a single soul around for miles. Now you and your children can do whatever you want.

Not so fast.

Act like wild animals on a hike, and you'll destroy the very aspects of the outdoors that make it so attractive. Act like wild animals, and you're likely to end up back in civilization, specifically an emergency room. And there are other people around. Just as you would wish them to treat you courteously, so you and your children should do the same for them.

So how do you act civilized out in the wilds?

Minimize damage to your surroundings

When on the trail, follow the maxim of "Leave no trace." Obviously, you shouldn't toss litter on the ground, start rockslides, or pollute water supplies. How much is damage and how much is good-natured exploring is a gray area, of course. Most serious backpackers will say you should never pick up objects, break branches, throw rocks, pick flowers, and so on – the idea is not to disturb the environment at all.

Good luck getting a four-year-old to think like that. The good news is a four-year-old won't be able to throw around many rocks or break many branches.

Still, children from their first hike into the wilderness should be taught to respect nature and to not destroy their environment. While you might overlook a preschooler hurling rocks into a puddle, they can be taught to sniff rather than pick flowers. As they grow older, you can teach them the value of leaving the rock alone. Regardless of age, don't allow children to write on boulders or carve into trees.

Many hikers split over picking berries. To strictly abide by the "minimize damage" principle, you wouldn't pick any berries at all. Kids, however, are likely to find great pleasure in eating blackberries, currants and blueberries as ambling down the trail. Personally, I don't see any problem enjoying a few berries if the long-term payoff is a respect and love for nature. To minimize damage, teach them to only pick berries they can reach from the trail so they don't trample plants or deplete food supplies for animals. They also should only pick what they'll eat.

Collecting is another issue. In national and most state and county parks, taking rocks, flower blossoms and even pine cones is illegal. Picking flowers moves many species, especially if they are rare and native, one step closer to extinction. Archeological ruins are extremely fragile, and even touching them can damage a site.

But on many trails, especially gem trails, collecting is part of the adventure. Use common sense – if the point of the trail is to find materials to collect, such as a gem trail, take judiciously, meaning don't overcollect. Otherwise, leave it there.

Sometimes the trail crosses private land. If so, walking around fields, not through them, always is best or you could damage a farmer's crops.

Pack out what you pack in

Set the example as a parent: don't litter yourself; whenever stopping, pick up whatever you've dropped; and always require kids to pick up after themselves when they litter. In the spirit of "Leave no trace," try to leave the trail cleaner than you found it, so if you come across litter that's safe to pick up, do so and bring it back to a trash bin in civilization. Given this, you may want to bring a plastic bag to carry out garbage.

Picking up litter doesn't just mean gum and candy wrappers but also some organic materials that take a long time to decompose and aren't likely to be part of the natural environment you're hiking. In particular, these include peanut shells, orange peelings, and eggshells.

Burying litter, by the way, isn't viable. Either animals or erosion soon will dig it up, leaving it scattered around the trail and woods.

Stay on the trail

Hiking off trail means potentially damaging fragile growth. Following this rule not only ensures you minimize damage but is also a matter of safety. Off trail is where kids most likely will encounter dangerous animals and poisonous plants. Not being able to see where they're stepping also increases the likelihood of falling and injuring themselves. Leaving the trail raises the chances of getting lost. Staying on the trail also means keeping out of caves, mines or abandoned structures you may encounter. They are usually dangerous places.

Finally, never let children take a shortcut on a switchback trail. Besides putting them on steep ground upon which they could slip, their impatient act will cause the switchback to erode.

Trail Dangers

On North Shore trails, two common dangers face hikers: ticks and poison ivy/sumac. Both can make miserable your time on the trail or once back home. Fortunately, both threats are easily avoidable and treatable.

Ticks

One of the greatest dangers comes from the smallest of creatures: ticks. Both the wood and the deer tick are common in Minnesota and can infect people with Lyme disease.

Ticks usually leap onto people from the top of a grass blade as you brush against it, so walking in the middle of the trail away from high plants is a good idea. Wearing a hat, a long sleeve shirt tucked into pants, and pants tucked into shoes or socks, also will keep ticks off you, though this is not foolproof as they sometimes can hook onto clothing. A tightly woven cloth provides the best protection, however. Children can pick up a tick that has hitchhiked onto the family dog, so outfit Rover and Queenie with a tick-repelling collar.

After hiking into an area where ticks live, you'll want to

examine your children's bodies (as well as your own) for them. Check warm, moist areas of the skin, such as under the arms, the groin and head hair. Wearing light-colored clothing helps make the tiny tick easier to spot.

To get rid of a tick that has bitten your child, drip either disinfectant or rubbing alcohol on the bug, so it will loosen its grip. Grip the tick close to its head, slowly pulling it away from the skin. This hopefully will prevent it from releasing saliva that spreads disease. Rather than kill the tick, keep it in a plastic bag so that medical professionals can analyze it should disease symptoms appear. Next, wash the bite area with soap and water then apply antiseptic.

In the days after leaving the woods, also check for signs of disease from ticks. Look for bulls-eye rings, a sign of Lyme disease. Other symptoms include a large red rash, joint pain, and flu-like symptoms. Indications of Rocky Mountain spotted fever include headache, fever, severe muscle aches, and a spotty rash first on palms and feet soles that spread, all beginning about two days after the bite.

If any of these symptoms appear, seek medical attention immediately. Fortunately, antibiotics exist to cure most tick-related diseases.

Poison ivy/sumac

Often the greatest danger in the wilds isn't our own clumsiness or foolhardiness but various plants we encounter. The good news is that we mostly have to force any encounter with flora.

Touching the leaves of either poison ivy or poison sumac in particular results in an itchy, painful rash. Each plant's sticky resin, which causes the reaction, clings to clothing and hair, so you may not have touched a leaf, but once your hand runs against the resin on shirt or jeans, you'll probably get the rash.

To avoid contact with these plants, you'll need to be able to identify each one. Remember the "Leaves of three, let it be" rule for poison ivy. Besides groups of three leaflets, poison ivy has shiny green leaves that are red in spring and fall. Poison sumac's leaves are not toothed as are non-poisonous sumac, and in autumn their leaves turn scarlet. Be forewarned that even after leaves fall off, poison oak's stems can carry some of the itchy resin.

By staying on the trail and walking down its middle rather than the edges, you are unlikely to come into contact with this pair of irritating plants. That probably is the best preventative. Poison ivy barrier creams also can be helpful, but they only temporarily block the resin. This lulls you into a false sense of safety, and so you may not bother to watch for poison ivy.

To treat poison ivy/sumac, wash the part of the body that has touched the plant with poison ivy soap and cold water. This will erode the oily resin, so it'll be easier to rinse off. If you don't have any of this special soap, plain soap somtimes will work if used within a half-hour of touching the plant. Apply a poison ivy cream and get medical attention immediately. Wearing gloves, remove any clothing (includeing shoes) that has touched the plants, washing them and the worn gloves right away.

For more about these topics and many others, pick up this author's **Hikes with Tykes: A Practical Guide to Day Hiking with Kids**. You also can find tips online at the author's **Day Hiking Trails** blog. Have fun on the trail!

Index

About the Author

Rob Bignell is a long-time hiker, journalist, and author of the popular "Hikes with Tykes," "Headin' to the Cabin," and "Hittin' the Trail" guidebooks and several other titles. He and his son Kieran have been hiking together for the past eight years. Before Kieran, Rob served as an infantryman in the Army National Guard and taught middle school students in New Mexico and Wisconsin. His newspaper work has won several national and state journalism awards, from editorial writing to sports reporting. In 2001, The Prescott Journal, which he served as managing editor of, was named Wisconsin's Weekly Newspaper of the Year. Rob and Kieran live in Wisconsin.

CHECK OUT THESE OTHER HIKING BOOKS BY ROB BIGNELL

"Headin' to the Cabin" series:
◆Day Hiking Trails of Northeast Minnesota
◆Day Hiking Trails of Northwest Wisconsin

"Hikes with Tykes" series:
◆Hikes with Tykes: A Practical Guide to Day Hiking
 with Children
◆Hikes with Tykes: Games and Activities

"Hittin' the Trail" series:
Minnesota
◆Interstate State Park (ebook only)
Wisconsin
◆Barron County
◆Bayfield County
◆Burnett County (ebook only)
◆Chippewa Valley (Eau Claire, Chippewa, Dunn, Pepin
 counties)
◆Crex Meadows Wildlife Area (ebook only)
◆Interstate State Park (ebook only)
◆Polk County (ebook only)
◆Sawyer County
National parks
◆Best Sights to See at America's National Parks
◆Grand Canyon (ebook only)

ORDER THEM ONLINE AT:
hikeswithtykes.com/hittinthetrail_home.html

GET CONNECTED!

Follow the author to learn about other great trails and for useful hiking tips…

Blog
hikeswithtykes.blogspot.com

Facebook
www.facebook.com/Day-Hiking-Trails-245054895514379

Google+
plus.google.com/collection/8OInb

LinkedIn
www.linkedin.com/in/robbignell

Pinterest
www.pinterest.com/rbignell41

Twitter
twitter.com/dayhikingtrails

Website
http://hikeswithtykes.com/hittinthetrail_home.html

WANT MORE INFO ABOUT FAMILY DAY HIKES?

Follow this book's blog, where you'll find:

Tips on day hiking with kids

Lists of great trails to hike with children

Parents' questions about
day hiking answered

Product reviews

Games and activities for the trail

News about the book series
and author

Visit online at:

hikeswithtykes.blogspot.com

Made in the USA
Middletown, DE
19 October 2022

13054881R00050